may i wear your crown

a collection of short poetry & prose by
christopher tapp

may i wear your crown

~ poetry & prose ~

by
christopher tapp

Book design by Olivier Tardif
Illustrations by Oak S.L.

content warning:

self-harm
suicidal ideation
sexual trauma
eating disorders
substance abuse
adult illustrations

praise for may i wear your crown

"*May I Wear Your Crown* is a devastatingly honest collection that will rip your heart open. Tapp is not afraid of going to vulnerable places, opening up about addiction and mental health in a way that lets you truly see them. Anyone who's gone through transformation in life can relate to and find solace in these deeply personal poems."

- Michaela Angemeer, bestselling author of 'you'll come back to yourself'

"Confident in its queerness, proud of its vulnerability, *May I Wear Your Crown* is a passionate exhale of emotions, a bold exploration of queer identity and mental health experiences that left me feeling liberated, 'seen', and above all, ready to begin working on my very own fairytale."

- Sam Payne, author of 'this boy is a rainbow'

"A raw, poignant examination of love, sexuality, addiction, and mental health—all with a shining undercurrent of hope. If you're looking for poetry that makes you feel seen with a perfect balance of pain and beauty, this collection is unwavering."

- Michelle Awad, author of 'Soul Trash, Space Garbage'

"There are some stories that just connect with you. They feel almost like they reach into your soul to find exactly what you need or what you've been through and it's such a cool reading experience. That's how I felt with this poetry collection."

- @readingwithamy, notable booktoker

"I started reading this book in the morning with my coffee, and I just kept coming back to it every morning. Each piece made me think abstractly. Tapp leaves his pieces with a question to the reader, which not only is engaging, it also makes the reader want to keep turning the pages."

- Maria Giesbrecht, author of 'Peeling Oranges'

"Enough of the sad endings for queer or mentally ill poets. Gone are the days when either of those things could be tolarated as a death sentence: poetry is a vessel for emotion, and joy is one of the most poignant. *may i wear your crown* shines in this genre of contemporary poetry, with its focus on strength as something which comes as much from community as it does from within."

- Ariane Beck, Goodreads reviewer

table of contents

when i look around
and can't find myself
i still see you
and everything i want to be

- *may i wear your crown*

prologue

i shattered. i crumbled. i lit a match & burned down my home. my own family. all the love. the trees. the buildings. i let myself & everything i've ever known turn to ash. without batting an eye. i took all the homophobia, all the punches, all the heartbreak, *the daddy issues*, the constant need for attention - i took it all out from the pit that lived inside of my stomach, & i let it combust. *explode.* destroy. committing arson on my entire life.

instead of healing, i decided to throw all of my hurt at the world. crying: *what did i do to deserve this?*

deciding to wither, i chose to be bitter. bought a box of party blowers & party hats then shouted: *let's celebrate taking pity on ourselves!*

i lived inside of that heartbreak & chaos for so long that i almost forgot who i was. what i stood for. who i wanted to be.
always looking for myself inside of other people.
finding comfort within the falling; i told myself i deserved everything bad that had ever happened to me.

so, this is the story of how i convinced myself otherwise.

how i convinced myself:

i am still magic.

may i
introduce
myself

it's okay to be
a little overgrown

there are golden people
that do exist
beyond the gates of your dreams
that will not only paint your skies
baby blue
and turn your clouds
into cotton candy
with their shining hands
they will have you feeling
like the warmest tea
when you need it most
on your coldest days
they will be there
because
there are golden people
that do exist

for my sister:

i clean the walls at work
daydreaming of golden earrings for me
and pearl necklaces for you

we are sipping cocktails (i'm not an alcoholic in my daydreams)
laughing about how angry other rich people are

they wish they had it like us

young and limitless
new to money, but old souls
you run a luxury day care now
and i recite poetry so we can afford these long beach chairs,
fake tans, and lip injections.
funny how they age some, but not us

your hair is so soft from the homemade shampoo recipe
the waitress at the country club gave us
do you think we should invite her out for drinks?
that's what nana would've liked for us to do
be courteous and grateful to those who give

stop talking about our dads
i say at least once a day
under this sun is where we bathe in our grace
you and i are the magic fraternal twins
hidden gems in society
we have mouths that are quiet
but minds that are as loud as lions

share your story
only
when you are ready

skipping stones at the quarry
sleeping in your old dodge
you mumble,
your music is boring

how will we ever get out of here
if we never stop drinking

it seems as though
we've jumped in the water
and are now just

sinking

sinking

sinking

i dream of things
bigger than myself
but then sit back
and watch them not happen

we need to be careful
about the lines we ~~cross~~
with our
affirmations
and mantras

manifest happiness and it will come
is a dangerous segue
into failure and let down

the prideful members
of my community's history
manifested nothing but
love
and more love
yet in exchange
got nightly
police raids

and now lives
are still
being taken
for spreading
anything short of
deep affection,
authenticity,
and warmth

how dark and pretty we are
like a fire fed by pixie dust
we are one of mother nature's
guiltiest pleasures

take me back to
when polaroids were cool,
dipping strawberries in chocolate,
and crying over
rose and jack dawson

we too
now have
oceans   between   us
but the growing apart
only makes us
grow closer

- *childhood best friend*

i moved away at eighteen. danced   in circles of smoke. kissed a
hundred new boys. i tried convincing myself that i was a beautiful
mess. yelled at my sister for existing. stole her car for blackout joy
rides. drank with friends. kissed my friends. felt free (because of my
friends). i created a world full of the quickest ecstasy. i ignored my
mother. blocked out her cries: screaming my name over and over.
crying my name. over and over. *come back home.* i thought growing
up meant i had to grow apart from something. had to be mysterious.
had to have a rock bottom story. *why do i glamorize death? why
do i wish for heartache? where does this need for pain come from?*

i am afraid of easy
non catastrophic love
of getting bored
from growing old
where is the show stopping
gut wrenching
never ending back and forth
gemini versus aries
not meant to be
so we rewrite destiny

where did all that
passion run and hide

even if time decided to start
flowing in reverse
we'd still be waiting
for what's next

please stop chipping away
at my truth
put down your pitchforks
and sharpened knives
i am not here to
shove my ways into your face
but nor am i here to hide
or play dress up
as a man who says
no to gay
but
yes to adultery

you and i
are not the same
but that does not
make us too different

the curtains are open
for each and every
one of us
this is our stage
this is our show

- *don't play the villain*

the world must start showing more kindness
to the women that were forced into single motherhood
reaching outwards left and right
for anything they could hold onto
for some support
sinking themselves for years
so their children could stay afloat

nobody plans to live by desperate measures

our mothers are our keepers
and they don't deserve anything
less than the highest of thrones

how can anyone not love
winter snow at night
shimmering as if fairies
flew by and emptied out
all their bags of
leftover magic

you are not doing
god's work
when you break
apart my love

i love my city
all the tiny stores
crammed together on each street
like a caterpillar forgot his own size
before forming his cocoon

i could hide amongst these bricks
until the earth sinks
the island down
they say the water is rising
but we choose to ignore it
or maybe we're all aware
but have dreams too big,
too fast paced,
to stop for the sea

like the construction here,
being done on every third block
this city taught me
that broken things
can be fixed,
even new things
can get redone

i love my city
we reinvent ourselves here
every month or so
alter egos,
name changes,
you pick it
you can have it

i love my city
and it loves me too

they did not
have permission
i'd lay barely awake
they did not
have permission
yet they would
take and take
my body
my thoughts
my soul
my words
anything that
would make
them feel like
the bigger man

i turned one hundred years old
on my twenty-first birthday
with enough dark history
to fill museums
for decades

i'm about five times
older than i look

all i am
is a prince
waiting for his prince

when did the war on love start

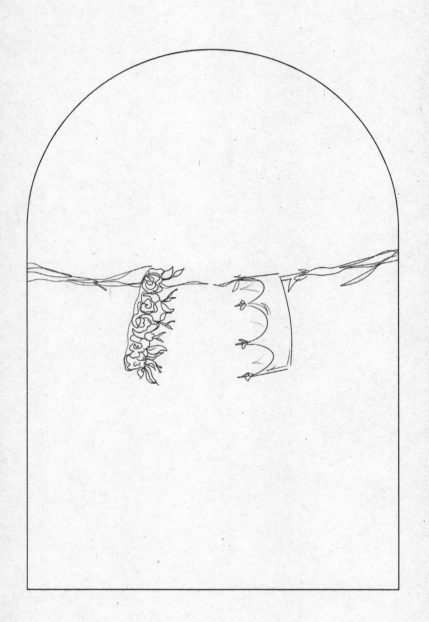

may
i be
your *
prince

my legs have teeth marks
where you should be
planting kisses

who ripped your throat open
and took out every last word
you've ever muttered
i love you
isn't a death wish
it is the beginning of
rewriting your own story

can we dance under the blankets,
each wear dazzling crowns,
and talk about how our softest parts
could build up the strongest empire
brick by brick with
glitter stained mortar

you can unleash yourself onto me
cast all the spells you'd like
trust me, nobody else is in these woods
cover my back with your sequins
paint my face with your gold adhesive

we can be innocent
we can be gentle
we can be soft
yet still be so wild
and give this forest
something to remain enchanted for

please tell me
if you ever start
to lose your own
voice for me
or skip over
topics for me
i am loving you
the only way
i've ever known
and been shown
how to love
and i can't tell
if that's enough

can we cut
out stars from
construction paper
and hang them
from the ceiling
with some old string
from the kitchen's
junk drawer
can we pour
glitter all over
the tables and
the chairs and
the floors
can we make
this empty house
s p a r k l e
like we do

i want a big gay movie
that doesn't end
with a lover's death
after a buildup of
hidden lustful romance
i want a hollywood blockbuster
of two women meeting
at the carnival
the notebook style
to eventually spend
the rest of their
dramatic lives together
happily married
with ten kids
i want a non-binary lead
on every cinema screen
showing us love is limitless
and exists beyond
society's norms and boundaries
i want a good queer film
can someone explain to me
why all the gay movies
are so damn depressing
can someone explain to me
why we are teaching
closeted teenagers
to stay unhappy

there is no wrong way
to let your heart
crack open
for love

press your chest
against mine
feel that warmth
we make together
it could strike up fires
big enough to burn
down forests

the way you live
so care free
caught me off guard
i'm constantly in
fight or flight mode

can you love someone
that is a little too
fickle for their own good
that can't decide on
which pronouns to use
they are always on
the edge of a relapse
singing off key
they don't ever
let anybody in
skipping at least
one meal a day
i guess what i'm
trying to ask is
can you love someone
that cannot love themselves

do you ever
get so sad that
you can't even
write about it

let's romanticize
dying flowers and lust,
kissing in the rain,
and one of us
drinking too much

let's romanticize
breaking each other's hearts
for no other reason than
we love the drama

let's fall apart
and only really
be in love
with each other
when we have to
fix the other

let's romanticize it all
until we are
        completely
             gone
                together

i want you
i really do
but i also
want what
you lack
i want to
lose control
and find comfort
inside of losing
myself with you
i want to be
with someone
who would die
at the thought
of losing me too

i cry when you leave
not because *i miss you already,*
but because i'm terrified
of being alone

when you think of me

please imagine

a full faced smile,
half emptied tea mugs,
a boy who can't sleep
until at least two a.m.,
a laugh that makes
your heart jump
when we'd watch
rudolph in june,
and the softest hair that
your fingers could ever swim through

do not forget the little things

do not forget why

you loved me

humour me, please

how am i so pretty to you,
when the world tells me
that i am undeserving
of anything beautiful

last night when you said you'd like to have me for dessert. you filled me up with trust and all things enticing. every time you took a bite; my body jolted a little closer to your thighs. always ready for the taking. *tie my arms behind my back, place an apple in my mouth, and feast on me like i'm your favourite meal.*

that melomaniac boy
always chasing dreams
bigger than himself
how can he not see
the best beat
and rhythm
is burning
in between my legs

- *right in front of you*

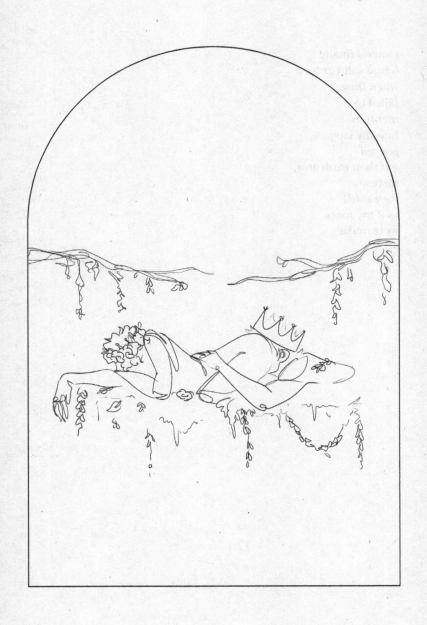

i knew i finally
found solid ground
when they
failed to
mention
how my laugh
popped
out their eardrums,
instead
they acted
as if my roars
were music

who needs a
higher power
when i can
just be on
my knees

worshipping you

i want to escape this city with you
using witchcraft
in the nearest woods
to shrink ourselves
into the size of pennies

we can make friends with local ants
and maybe they'll help us
build a home by a stream
that'll seem like an ocean
from our perspective

and to pay the colony back
for their grace
you can teach them music
and i can start a poetry workshop
letting them know
that we are all allowed
to express ourselves

with fireflies dancing
above our bed
and
fairies making homes
out of nearby stumps

we are an enchanted love

i wish i didn't care so much
about how my stomach looks
when the lights aren't dimmed

do you see
these arms
the ones you call *petite*
are the biggest bones
that i have ever seen

let me draw
your taurus sun
by connecting your
back freckles
how does your skin
shimmer like that
under the two p.m. sky
on another average day
you are still pure magic

they don't make pure hearts anymore
not like the one you speak with
in the bottom of your throat
i can hear it breaking
every time you try
to stutter your
truth

pick me up
like pixie dust
sprinkle me on
your softest parts
and remember our love
is magic

your voice is
waves crashing
on old footprints
left in the sand
washing away
anything that
came before you
is now insignificant

i'd permanently live
on your hip bones
if you'd let me

my arms outstretched
to the ceiling fan
both my almond eyes
staring down into yours: deep blue

i can almost touch heaven from up here

of course i am
the jealous type
this world
brought me up saying
you will never be enough

do you feel my hands sweat
when my voice cracks
because all i see
is unfinished art
spread out on our sheets
waiting to be
something new
something beautiful
something worth a gaze
a double look
or its own gallery

you've been around for a lot of my good days
but on days like today
when my heart feels too heavy
to carry out our love
i'll put my phone on silent
and sink into my mattress
trying not to drink depanneur wine
i log onto an a.a. meeting
or three
with my cat tugging
to get under the blankets
he too knows this is the only safe spot
no distractions
we just sleep and cry under here
because on days like today
the bad days
i'd rather see you in my dreams
where i'm productive
instead of in this half functional reality

- on days i don't believe in magic

on days I don't believe in magic

thank you for reminding me
that i am capable of
being loved,
despite my
past

let yourself
believe in fairytales
and pixie dust
because magic
is the only thing
we can hold onto
when this world
seems so dark

dear boys,

i do not need a knight in shining armour. you can wrap my smallness up. *very easily, yes.* but that does not make me fragile or broken. so, please arrive with peace. leave your battle wounds and swords under the bridge, ahead of your arrival. no need to prepare for a duel. the dragon that lives here has grown to be my friend. so, please only approach the gate with kindness. i have no time for anything less. no need for any mindless heroics. i'll be patiently waiting for my prince (someone to be completely equal with).

sincerely,
the one who doesn't need saving

Sincerely,
the one who
doesn't need saving

i can live
a happily ever after
without you as my prince
but that does not mean
that i want to

i made love to myself
and to you
at the same time

i didn't know i could do that

i used to keep
my eyes closed
during sex
i'd be too
scared to giggle
too tense to
enjoy myself or
pleasure myself
too misused
to know that
i am allowed
to feel good
i am allowed
to scream
more!
i am allowed
to look the
way i look
i am allowed
to feel sexy
to dig my nails
into a consenting
partner
he
she
they
are allowed to
want me like
they've never wanted
anything before
we are allowed
to desire
the other
and not be
shy about it

- sexual lessons part 1

how did you take my entire existence
and turn it into something
entirely new

can you stir up some of that magic you hold
and make everyday a sunday
so we can forever wake up like this
no more nine to five or three to nine
no more dying for them
when we could be living for us

i see fields and fields of blue hydrangeas
where your eyes are supposedly resting
i just want to jump inside of them
and forever be within your sight

this is home
this is soft
this is where the sun learned how to rise
beauty is born here
and i can't afford to miss another minute of it

there are kaleidoscopes
all around your face

i now understand
what being rich feels like

what's braver than
letting yourself
trip over lust,
stuttering three words
with shaky knees,
completely naked

i love you

may, i
strike
a match

but tell me what happened that night
how did i wake up in your driveway
with half a bottle of pills
and my sister's car keys

why do we have a blackout love?
why do we destroy each other?

wrap my smallness up
like the fetish you have
for light and bright
air headed boys

there is an entire black hole
that lives permanently
inside of my gut

you left an empty wine glass
on my coffee table.
i've been refilling it
every day
just in case *you*
wanted to stop by,
for another sip of *us*

it's 4:26 a.m.
you've been gone now for three days
and i just woke up from a nightmare

it's 4:45 a.m.
and i can't stop staring at your empty side of the bed
you always knew how to calm me down

it's 5:15 a.m.
i find myself calling your number
but i hang up after one ring

it's now 6:13 a.m.
and i'm wondering if anybody
will ever be able to make me feel
as warm as you did
on the coldest nights

it's 8:00 a.m.
i made some black coffee for you
out of habit
and i'm sitting here with my tea
hoping you'll come join me soon

christopher tapp

i sought out
refuge in you
but all you did
was plant bombs
inside of my chest

with dignity,
i shatter for you
over and over
leaving behind
a dazzling trail
made from glitter stained glass

heartbreak hearts

but with you

it is always beautiful

remember how my back looked
glowing in the crystal lamp light
how soft and devastating
my moans were
every drunken night

eleven years old
in the bathtub
wondering
how long can i hold my breath
before my lungs give out

- when the sinking started

the safest place
i can think of
existing is
outside
myself

i can't stop drinking
him out of me
the way wine tastes
soothes me almost
as much as he did
giving me nearly enough
numbness to forget
how the love aches
everyday inside of my chest

your jeans always
had tiny pieces
of old weed in
the front pockets
and your kiss always
tasted like cheap
burnt coffee from
the gas station
you worked at
you were always
so ready to
fall apart but
still strong enough
to hold me together

loving you was

constant dreaming

constant hoping

constant pleading

constantly giving away my power
for nothing in return

missing you is

constant hunger

constant aching

constant numbing

constantly wishing to be anywhere
as long as anywhere is with you

i speak most often
of how warm they were
as if i'm choosing to forget
the coldness that they became

if i had superpowers
or a little bit of
some actual magic
flowing inside of me
i'd want to fly
myself to
neverland
or
far far away
maybe to the world
that only exists
deep inside
the wardrobe
or the island
with the wild ones
some place where
the riptides don't
take me under
some place where
rock bottom
doesn't exist
even if i
had magical powers
i'd still be trying
to escape my life

so maybe
the cutting
the pills
and the tantrums were
all for attention
but that doesn't make them
any less real

it only means
we found a reason
for why they happened

- *loneliness (a cry for help)*

thank you for loving me
as long as you could have

i know it wasn't easy

i'm pleading guilty and i know it's too late
but thanks for picking up the phone at 2 a.m.
i just wanted you to know that i am guilty
of not loving you when i should have
and only now realizing that every part of me
functions as a half without you
and i know that you know
all of this hurt i'm feeling
is what you felt with me
and i'm sorry i didn't plead guilty earlier
or take the time to cup your tears
and look inside of them for answers
instead i called you crazy and delusional
for pushing me away
when *i'm perfect*
i really thought that
i read every single self help book, after you left
and convinced myself the stars shined just for me
and this world would fall apart if i fell apart
but then i did fall apart
i was gone
a sad replacement of myself
i was hollow
so i'm pleading guilty
and i guess some things never change
because i'm holding on to the hope
that the outcome of me pleading guilty
will result in my gut
not feeling so empty anymore
so if i can't have you back
after confessing my wrongs
then please do me a favour (i know you don't owe me one)
but for old times sake
can you just give me
the other half
of my heart back?

i like to pretend
we were together longer
than we really were

it makes me feel
less guilty about being
this sad over you

wild things

wild things

wild things

tell me,
why do i
only feel safe
buried deep
inside of
chaos

caress and
undress me
like you
used to do
or leave the
door open
for someone
who will

it's good to hear
your heart beat again
but why is it
so loud now

who gave you what i couldn't?

was i exoctic to you?
a dip your toe in chaos
type of love
just to make your
mommy and daddy mad
you licked and bit both
of my thighs
like they were
drenched in poison
when all along
you were the serpent

just forty-five more crunches away from happiness
twenty-five more push ups away from self-respect
fifteen more squats and maybe he'll stay
maybe he'll love me, even
and i'll be fine
for today, at least
the best v-line
a muscled up back
a rib cage that screams
i'm hungry
a face that screams
i'm dizzy
but at least
i'm attractive
sweating and sweating
the self-hate
right out of me
no need for rest days
when today could be
our best day yet
to show them
how hard we work
to prove our worth
i am immaculate
i am resilient
i am not lying to myself
i will feel good tomorrow
this pain will be worth it

- *my workout routine*

i think my lungs
are now as black
as the coffee i have
every morning
without you

after one year and a half of silence, freedom from the constructs, and spare time to be with me, i walk around the city i used to know. the city i loved. the city i now feel nostalgic about. the city i left behind without ever leaving. moments i wasn't awake for on every second street and seventeenth avenue. the dizzy laughs and unfocused street lights. *how can i go back? where is the music? where is my city?*

where is my city?

how can i
shrink
shrink
shrink
quickly
into a size small enough
for the world's attention

how did my body and i
end up here again
caught up in the middle of
this dysmorphic-love-turmoil
when did the recovering stop
and the hatred creep in
was it before or after they said
you look so much better toned
how much did they analyze
my slimness before
and when did they decide
what would equate to me
being the *perfect* sculpt?

i have a stomach ache
and a fever.
my mom said
to just take a nap
but my mind wanders: *google, tell me*
          what are the early signs
          of stomach cancer

i've got a new mole
on my right thigh
it's kind of opaque, *google, tell me*
          what does skin cancer
          feel like
          or look like

my bottom row's gums
have been receding, *google, tell me*
          am i too young
          to develop a
          gum disease

i've got a new rash
on my right shoulder
my chest is red, too
and my heart's been
beating fast
it might just be the caffeine
or the anxiety
or both
or it could be
a heart attack

i've been
struggling
to breathe, *google, tell me*
          what are the
          symptoms of dying

- *hypochondriac*

i've always been *cute*
never sexy or desired
but just
good enough
to hold hands with
or to be seen
on a date with
but not mysterious enough
(a little too talkative)
 to have a second round
of drinks with
i've always been *cute*
but i've never
been craved

just one crushed up pill
almost had me
forgetting his voice
so please give me
the whole damn bottle
and watch me
never speak of
that boy again

how much wine must i drink
to get the sour taste
of your kiss
off of my lips
and out from beneath my tongue

i keep thinking strangers look just like you
or they might not even look like you at all
but my mind wants you so bad
that it forges your face onto theirs
without my slightest bit of consent

the overdose does not define you

the overdose does not define you

the overdose does not define you

but how can my rock bottom
not define my every move?

the drinking for me
was the loving i never got from those who should've provided it
it was the affirmations my therapist told me to practice in the mirror
it was the, *you are enough*, from every boy that ended up leaving
it was the only safe spot in a small town full of violence
the drinking was what half of my heart missed
it made up for the social anxiety, depression
anything the psychiatrist could label me with next
drinking cured that

i had a voice again. i was writing my best material.
drinking made me
entertaining
chris? oh, he's just the fun one.
the social butterfly.
the one to blackout with on friday
and reminisce with on saturday
about how we had so much fun last night
we did have fun last night, right?

drinking for me
filled the empty hole in my chest that i was too cold to deal with
so instead it's wine glasses laced with g.h.b
rum and coke but extra rum, please
beer bottles laced with guilt
i'm so sick of feeling guilty
someone just take this guilt, please
i'm on both knees
so drinking for me,

well drinking for me fixes everything
but nothing all at once
like they'd say in math class
two negatives makes a positive
so let me add every rock bottom into pairs
and wait for that miracle
12 steps forwards
12 steps backwards
this is too much work for somebody who loves instant fixing
when i already know what can fix me
i just need one more fix, please

you told me that
i was a hurricane

you told me that
i craved danger

you told me that
i wanted to be
taken advantage of

and i kept on
believing you

- *manipulator*

you cannot give
proper consent
if you are
blackout
drunk

i failed grade ten math
took the class four times
but yet i've somehow
always managed to
perfect the art
of subtraction

we were so soft together
too tender to last
that even easy rain
could have broken what we had

there are certain words i say
differently now
because of you
i sound a little bit like us
and the language we made together
and i hate that
because i don't want
to ever have you
in my mouth again

may i
take
a breath

you will learn to live with it
what the triggers are
and how to find peace
with this gap in your heart

i picture us everyday
how we could've been
standing in the sun
drinking champagne
without me starting a fight
dipping our feet
into the clearest water
we've ever seen
right before leaving
footprint trails that intertwine
on the sand's surface

but then my imagination stops

the story just stops

because that version
of life isn't real
and neither are we

writing about you after you've left is a bittersweet release. it's a lump in the throat type of writing. leaving my bones crushed in ink. these are long lost cousins to the love poems that once carried your name. with every syllable. my journals bleed the words that wrote the story of us. each locked diary has hidden their key from me. they cannot stand any more plot twists to the folk tale about the lonely prince. our guards are up. and my gut is whispering. *it is okay to put down the pen. take a deep breath. and rest.*

our love will
forever live
down by the old port

things heartbreak taught me:

1. i love so deeply, my chest cracks
2. i drink too much wine
3. i am codependent
4. cats cuddle better than boys
5. vegan ice cream counts as a friend
6. black coffee makes the days shorter
7. yoga doesn't fix everything
8. some doors must stay shut
9. i am the jealous type
10. i have a lot of triggers
11. my friends don't blackout when they drink
12. my friends are my family
13. i am powerful

i am every shooting star
you'll ever miss,
from always looking in
the wrong direction

i built the foundation of my recovery
with broken bottles,
scotch tape
and sticky corks,
the floors and walls may seem unsteady
a tad too creaky
for your liking
but that is just fine with me
because my sobriety
is not a one size fits all thrifted tee
that gets passed on down from dad to son
it is a map of tunnels leading me through
rock bottom to clear skies

- *my sobriety does not belong to you*

my sobriety does not belong to you

you can slow down
yet still be productive

i think i'm starting to love the calm
and the idea of staying in it forever
instead of momentarily resting
in the calm after the storm

i don't want comedowns anymore

no more dark clouds or sad poetry

maybe they'll think
i'm out of my mind
or that i have no idea
what reality is
but they would be wrong
because i have used up my nine lives
and have been given a tenth chance at happiness
a tenth chance with hope
for living in the now

and i don't intend on wasting it

twenty two birthday cakes. a high school break up. an adulting break up. an i-dropped-out-of-school party. a daily serenity prayer. and a love letter to myself (apologizing for your absence). yet i'm still always questioning: *could i have prevented it? is it too late to reach back out?* you want to be my friend. but i don't need new friends. i work with enough strangers. strangers that haven't spent their lives sitting in the backseat of trouble-in-paradise. red lights. blue lights. you were busy. you missed it all. every glimpse of growth that sprouted my power. you cannot keep walking through old doors and expecting them to remain open. after years. and years. new locks have been installed. yellow trimmings you wouldn't recognize. it is bright in here. *i raised myself up.* she said you hope i'm happy. i very much am. spitting image of you but with the best plot twist ever written. *this* version of your face knows how to smile. listen. apologize. *this* version of you knows how to love. and knows how to shine.

stop wishing to forget
a story that taught you
so many lessons

he only wanted parts of you
as if you were a tree with
no branches or leaves
now that isn't love, my dear
that is self-seeking, self-serving
you are not a safe spot
to just keep him warm

you are an entire home

he cannot seek hibernation in you
like a squirrel does in winter

when the leaves start to fall
he must be there to catch them
and wrap you up with warmth
after they are all gone

that is what love should be like

stop hiding behind butterflies,
sad sad metaphors,
and words dressed up in flowers

you are wholeheartedly exceptional
and your honesty will prove that

his absence left a hole in me
bigger than the one
left in my lungs at birth
but i now know
what healing looks like

it's four group meetings a day for me
and a phone call to my sister
just to say *i love you*

but despite all the power
i wear now
like armour on a knight
i wish my departed prince
could've met me
after the healing

- *wrong timing love*

i am allowed
to want to be
swept up off
of my feet

my greatest power lives inside of my words

so maybe
i do love chaos
and stories
that end
in a great spiral
of tragedy
and ache
but i also love
quick kisses
to say goodbye
in the morning
and cold coffee
when it's with
someone i love
i might dream
of being empty
but i also dream
of being full

i moved to the small town
just outside the city we built together
it is little
quiet
very peaceful
and has no traces of him
in its royal blue and cherry red houses

the sidewalks are cleaner too
and sorbet is really popular here
the villagers around
told me that i am
the warmest creature
to have rolled in from foreign land
but they also said that i make no sense
when i ramble on about the little prince
giving me all my warmth
because it almost sounded like
i needed him
more than i needed myself

as if i couldn't build an entire city alone
or a tower to the stars on my own

to my fellow addicts (a love letter),

for when you feel like using again: crack open your favourite flavour of sparkling water, and remind yourself that urges or relapses do not mean you are failing. sit back, watch the rain fall, and list down all your favourite things about yourself. you may feel as though you have no favourite parts. it may feel as though you're washed up and are only made of all things unloveable - but that is wrong. you are glowing. you are accomplished. you are breathing (and that is a victory all on it's own). so, when you feel like using or abusing your power: place your palms over your chest and feel your heartbeat. feel the life that swims through you ready to continue and try. feel the life that you were strong enough to give another day to. nobody around you might understand the cravings but that does not mean you are alone. *i am here.* the sober community is here. all different paths. all different stories. but the same struggles. the same urges. and the same hope. a hope that rock bottom is just living underneath something. underneath the light. beneath the neverending sprouting roots. and above it all is your power, waiting to grow.

i am a soul
i am a body
i am a breath
i am a moment
i am everything
i've ever wanted

i found out that love hides
in the most unexpected places
like in my
cat's eyes during chin rubs

love pops out of the mail drop box
after i shoot down a letter
i get tingles

love hides in the air
and hides in our fingertips

magic is real
it lives where
love lives

isn't it funny how
i thought i was starving
i thought i was empty
without someone saying
they love me

but the love has
always been here

it's been waiting
for me everywhere

the right one will not ask
for you to give up your home
or hand over your softness
they will simply ask
may we share this space
and be soft together

celebrate your favourite holidays by pumpkin carving, with mocktails and smiles. celebrate the sunrises, sunsets, and all the new moments in between. celebrate your friends on their birthdays, bad days, and every day in between. celebrate sex, masturbation, or self-empowering abstinence. celebrate your body. celebrate food. celebrate the joy, the love, and even the darkness. give the ache a place to rest. light up sparklers for every occasion. celebrate it all. because all that you have, and all that you are, is worth the grandest of celebrations.

- you are a gift

when your close friends
say that they are
worried about you
you should
really listen

my sponsor asked me
to name my addiction
so i named him Blue
because his favourite time to visit
is when the sun has set
and i am all alone
bathing in cold nostalgia
with a tear filled bathtub

Blue has a funny way of expressing love
he brings me the most tender euphoria
but plucks out all of my softest parts

if i could keep Blue under a pillow
and only taste him at night
then i would do that forever
but he only likes me for himself
and i deserve more
than a selfish
destructive love

if you are in the midst
of healing and letting go
try to make sure
the energy around you
is reflecting that growth

i am sorry
to the gay kid
i laughed at
at christian camp
before i knew
i was gay too
i'm sorry that i
split your world
right in half
so i could
form my own
i'm sorry i
made you feel
like you were
a sin

you are not a sin

love your community

the fairytale is over
and i'm overlooking the city
remembering what made
that story so damn magical

it wasn't the boy
or the fairies
or even the way
the world felt brighter

it was me

it was me being
the truest part of it all
always remaining faithful
and humble
and honest
and never letting
his opinions change my views

i was the magic
growing
recognizing my worth
i began the first chapter
as beautiful
and closed the book
even more stunning

- *i was the whole damn fairytale*

the entire universe exists inside of me

you were home
when no boy could hold me
you kept my secrets guarded
relapse after relapse
with friends checking out
as often as i blinked
you gave me permission

to feel whatever i needed
to feel as loud as i wanted

- *dear diary*

to all the old and new
golden arms that have
reached out to embrace me
i cherish you now
and i will cherish you always

this is where magic
was born
then died
this is where love
was found
then lost
this is where i
felt hope
and light
and peace
within the chaos
this is where
i poured myself
out completely
so i could
be regrown

~ the end ~

acknowledgements

to every single person that has followed & encouraged me along on this journey of self expression. to all the new internet friendships i have formed (thanks to the beautiful & ever growing online poetry community). to my boyfriend, Olivier, for letting me publish sappy poems about him & also for turning my book visions into reality (he's the book designer, you guys!). to Kelsey & Sam for always being so patient with me & teaching me so much about life (you saved me without even realizing it). to Myriam for literally being my kindred spirit. to Jac for teaching me about the magic in being adventurous. to Virginia for showing me how to embrace & balance out my wild. & most importantly, to all of you reading this, thank you for adding me to your beautiful collection of books. i truly hope you opened this collection with an open heart and finished it learning something new about yourself or the world around you. i love you all. thank you. let's do this again sometime!

xoxo,
chris

about the author

christopher tapp is a writer of poetry, affirmations, and prose. they currently live in montreal, with their boyfriend and their two black cats, where they are also studying interior decorating & feng shui. their goal with all their work is to bring harmony into people's lives. *may i wear your crown* is the debut release from the author after a life long admiration of writing & storytelling. some topics they write about include love & heartbreak, addiction, sobriety, self discovery, and LGBTQ2+ issues.

find more of them on instagram & tiktok:
@chris.t.poetry